BRITISH RAILWAYS
IN THE 1950s AND '60s

Greg Morse

SHIRE PUBLICATIONS

Published in Great Britain in 2012 by Shire Publications Ltd,
Midland House, West Way, Botley, Oxford OX2 0PH,
United Kingdom.

44-02 23rd Street, Suite 219, Long Island City, NY 11101,
USA.

E-mail: shire@shirebooks.co.uk   www.shirebooks.co.uk

© 2012 Greg Morse.

A CIP catalogue record for this book is available from the
British Library.

Shire Library no. 699.   ISBN-13: 978 0 74781 168 8

Greg Morse has asserted his right under the Copyright,
Designs and Patents Act, 1988, to be identified as the
author of this book.

Page layout by Myriam Bell Design, UK and typeset in
Perpetua and Gill Sans.

Printed in China through Worldprint Ltd.

12 13 14 15 16   10 9 8 7 6 5 4 3 2 1

COVER IMAGE
The young fireman looks on as ex-GWR 4-6-0 no. 6870
Bodicote Grange backs onto its train at Oxford in 1964. The
locomotive would be withdrawn the following year; the
semaphores would last till the 1970s, when multi-aspect
colour light signalling came to the city.

TITLE PAGE IMAGE
Early BR splendour as ex-LMS 'unrebuilt Scot' no. 46148
The Manchester Regiment takes a Carlisle–Glasgow service
past Harthope in July 1953.

CONTENTS PAGE IMAGE
Changing of the guard. AL1 electric E3005 prepares to leave
Crewe in June 1964 as Sulzer Type 2 D5073 stands by. In
the background, ex-LMS 3F 0-6-0T no. 47391 is on pilot
duties.

DEDICATION
British Railways in the 1950s and '60s is dedicated to David,
Derek F., Derek H., Gerald, Graham, John, Philip, Michael
and Roger – the railway friends and colleagues who helped
make it possible.

ACKNOWLEDGEMENTS
I am indebted to Julia Jenkins, Mike Ashworth, Roger
Badger, David Brown, Paul Chancellor (Colour-Rail), John
Chalcraft (Rail Photoprints), David Christie, Great Central
Railwayana Auctions, D. J. Fleming, Graham Floyd, John
Foster, Derek Hotchkiss, Philip Hunt, Irene Grabowska,
Colin J. Marsden, Gerald Riley, Barry Toper (Transport
Treasury), Suzanne Faith, Michael Woods and STEAM
Museum, Swindon. Finally, I thank Nick Wright and
Russell Butcher at Shire Publications for making this book
so enjoyable to work on.

Illustrations are acknowledged as follows:
Mike Ashworth Collection, pages 12 (top), 22 (bottom),
23, 30 (bottom), and 37 (top); Hugh Ballantyne/
railphotoprints.co.uk, page 34; the late Alan H.
Bryant/railphotoprints.co.uk, pages 25 and 28 (top);
David Christie, cover and pages 3, 26, 39, and 40; David
Cobbe/railphotoprints.co.uk, pages 1, 7 (top), and 44
(top); Colour-Rail.com Collection, pages 6 (bottom), 8,
24 (bottom), 35, 38, 41 (top and bottom), and 49 (top);
Getty Images, page 4; Great Central Railwayana Auctions,
page 15 (top); John E. Henderson/colour-Rail.com, page
48; Mike Jefferies/railphotoprints.co.uk, page 44
(bottom); David A. Lawrence/colour-Rail.com, page 6
(top); Richard Lewis/railphotoprints.co.uk, page 46
(bottom); Railphotoprints.co.uk collection, pages 7
(bottom), 16, 20 (bottom), 24 (top), and 47; M. J.
Reade/colour-Rail.com, page 5; R. C. Riley/Transport
Treasury, page 18; Brian Robbins/railphotoprints.co.uk,
page 37 (bottom); David Rostance/railphotoprints.co.uk,
page 42; Science and Society Picture Library, pages 17 and
46 (top); STEAM Picture Library, pages 22 (top), 27, 28
(bottom), 31, 32, 33, 36, and 53; TheRailwayCentre.com,
page 50 (top) and 51 (bottom); Roy E. Vincent/Transport
Treasury, pages 11, 13, 15 (bottom), 16, and 20 (top); the
late Colin Whitfield/railphotoprints.co.uk, pages 29 and
45; the late R. A. Whitfield/railphotoprints.co.uk, page
21. All other images are from the author's collection.

Shire Publications is supporting the Woodland Trust, the UK's leading woodland conservation charity, by funding the dedication of trees.

CONTENTS

INTRODUCTION: TRANSITION THROUGH TIME

Opposite:
The Great Hall,
Euston, with
George
Stephenson's
statue surveying
the scene. Opened
in 1849, it had
become a dark,
uninviting place by
1950. This picture
was taken after
BR's refurbishment
of 1953. Sadly,
all would be
demolished
within a decade.

1950

A CRISP DECEMBER MORNING, and a black cab pulls up in Drummond Street beneath a glowing winter sun. A gloved hand pays the fare, a gnarled hand opens the door, and the silk-stockinged leg of a woman appears as she steps on to the London pavement. Her dark blue coat caressed by the breeze, she walks beneath the Doric Arch, across the courtyard and into the cathedral-like Great Hall. *Goodness, there are so many people! All milling around and getting in my way. But where is Hamish? I distinctly told him ... No wait, there he is – over by the statue.*

Janey waves gaily; Hamish waves back from his spot next to George Stephenson, happy that he's managed to buy the tickets already. There should be plenty of room on the train – they might even get a compartment to themselves if they're lucky. A porter, the brass buttons on his serge uniform shining, loads their luggage on to a trolley – presents for the aunts, presents for the nephews, and enough gowns and suits for a week of wining and dining in Scotland's second city. *Now, where's our platform? Gosh, Euston can be such a gloomy, smoky place...*

Just ahead, young Johnny unwraps his third toffee. He likes the departure side of the station the best. There's nothing like the sight of a steam train starting its journey – the plume of white smoke, the quickening bark of the exhaust, the slip of a wheel, the hiss of the sander – nothing like it on earth! Johnny worships the engine drivers and hopes to follow in his father's footsteps to become one himself. One day.

The porters and inspectors all know him – holidays and weekends, he'll be there, notebook and pencil in hand, Ian Allan *ABC* in his pocket. Sometimes they let him keep his penny platform ticket –

Below: Ex-LMS 'Duchess' Pacific no. 46235 *City of Birmingham* arrives at Euston with the 'Royal Scot' as parcels, packages and passenger await. This locomotive is preserved and resides at Thinktank, Birmingham's science museum.

5

Until 1962, the start of a journey from Euston looked like this; Philip Hardwick's magnificent Doric Arch was erected for the London & Birmingham Railway in 1837 as a triumphant gateway to the Midlands.

a trophy of his spoils, which he carefully places in an old tobacco tin at home. Occasionally, a driver will let him climb on to the footplate. Today, Old Charlie – a friend of his father at Camden Shed – gives him the tip. He doesn't need asking twice and soon finds himself basking in the welcome heat of no. 46256 *Sir William A. Stanier, F.R.S.* – a huge 'Pacific' named after its designer, though built under his successor George Ivatt and wearing the new black livery of British Railways. Johnny knows all this and more (much more!) thanks to his father, and the occasional copy of *The Railway Magazine* that his granddad gives him. He stands back as the fireman fills up the back corners of the grate, his metal shovel clanging as coal falls into flame. The driver checks his gauges and makes one or two deft adjustments before looking at his watch: 9.55 – just five minutes to go. Johnny knows it's time for him to leave – the 'Royal Scot' should never be late.

Back on the platform, he runs to the front of the train to savour the sight of the locomotive. How splendid it looks against the sky! *Sir William* is a 'cop' too – an engine he's never seen before, which means a lovely, long name to underline in the book tonight. All the same, he can't help wondering which member of the class will take over at Carlisle ...

A group of nuns, a young family, an old couple – *Ah, here we are!* Janey opens the door of the empty compartment and sets about adjusting it to her requirements, dropping the blind on one side, turning up the heat, and

Walking through the Arch would bring you to this courtyard, whence access to the station proper could be gained.

The 'Duchesses' had charge of the 'Royal Scot' throughout the 1950s and into the early 60s. In this 1956 view, no. 46222 *Queen Mary* is about to be turned at Kingmoor shed, locomotive changes usually being made at nearby Carlisle Citadel station.

opening the toplight a touch. These old carriages are past their best now, but they're warm, and their upholstery is soft and inviting. Outside, Hamish tips the porter and climbs aboard. Finding his wife, he kisses her and heads for the restaurant car, smiling as he sees a boy on the platform – at his age, he'd wanted to be an engine driver too. Perhaps he still does – just a little.

Ten o'clock comes: a lever is pulled and a green light shines; a guard's whistle blows and a green flag waves; the regulator opens and the engine breathes low. Passengers feel a jolt as the journey begins; Johnny's heart jumps at this stirring sight again.

He watches the train fight its way up Camden Bank til the tail lamp disappears. It's a timeless scene which will never change. Or so he thinks.

Diesels would soon start to make their presence felt at Euston. 'On the blocks' in July 1963 is D301, an English Electric Type 4 – the most powerful of the Pilot Scheme classes. In the background, the old departure platforms have been bulldozed in readiness for rebuilding.

7

1969

Euston had expanded haphazardly over the years and was blighted by a track layout that made it difficult to operate. The LMS had wanted to remodel the site in the 1930s, but the Second World War put paid to its plans. By the mid-1950s, BR knew it had to modernise: its assets had been seriously overworked and under-maintained during the war, and it needed to attract people away from planes and private cars.

The efficiencies and economies offered by electrification led to a scheme to upgrade the important route linking London with Birmingham, Manchester and Liverpool – building a new railway on top of the old, as someone put it. Yet the plans had no place for the Doric Arch and the Great Hall. The poet John Betjeman was active in the campaign to save the former, but all arguments were lost and site clearance began in 1961. Opened seven years later, the new Euston was, to some, a cold place that seemed to ignore passengers.

Johnny – or John as he now called himself – mused on all this from the cab of E3122, a sleek AL6 class electric locomotive, built in 1965. It seemed so long ago that he'd watched the great steam-hauled expresses leave from this same platform – although it was hardly the same platform now, truth be told. Back then, he'd thrilled to the sights, sounds and smells all around him, and delighted in the warmth of the footplate – especially on a cold day. When he started on the railway in 1957, modernisation was in the air, though there was still plenty of steam to be seen; like many

AL3 E3033 arrives at Euston in April 1967 with a rake of 'Mark II' coaches in BR's new corporate livery, as AL6 E3107 waits to depart. The blocks of flats in the background are a reminder that it wasn't just the railway that modernised in the 1950s and '60s.

others, he thought it would go on forever. But gone now are the puff of smoke and hiss of the injector; going now is the characteristic clickety-clack as jointed rails are replaced by welded ribbons of steel for a smoother, quieter ride. Goodness knows what Dad would have made of it all! At least the working conditions are cleaner, John thinks as he straightens his tie, sits back and checks his watch. Quarter to – not long now. And the 'Manchester Pullman' should never be late.

A platform ticket, costing 3d, entitling those meeting, waving off – or writing down engine numbers – to one hour on the station.

Keith pulls up in a taxi with time to spare. He soon finds the escalators, which raise him from the exhaust fumes of the basement to the bright, airy concourse above. Aunt Jane and Uncle Hamish aren't sure about the new Euston, but Keith likes the modern colours and clean lines. Perhaps that's Kathy's influence. Kathy, his girlfriend, teaches at the Manchester College of Art and Design. She likes modern colours and clean lines. She's the reason for Keith's trip today. He'd thought about driving – a zip up the new motorway and off at Rotherham, but this 'ton-up' Inter-City line is faster than the measly 70-mph M1. Why the 'Pullman'? *Well, why not?*

His ticket obtained from the Travel Centre, Keith checks the departures board, weaves round the commuters and heads for the Sprig Buffet. Sitting at a table, he allows his mind to wander. It's fairly quiet here, only the announcements shattering the solitude. He sips at a coffee, lights up another Embassy and meditates on the sculpture of Britannia that used to be in the old Great Hall. *She looks more at home here against the rich green felt,* he thinks, *a real touch of class.*

The rebuilt Euston Station in 1968. This artist's impression of the station concourse is taken from a booklet BR produced to mark the upgrade.

On the platform, two boys survey the scene, noting numbers here and there. The older lad loves steam and is getting bored with these electrics: they hardly make a sound; there's no *rhythm* to them. Camden Shed might have closed, but at least the old Roundhouse still has rhythm. He saw Pink Floyd there last month, and the more he thinks about it, the more fed up with trainspotting he feels. Soon, the lure of girls and guitars will take him away for good (or at least for thirty years or so, until the need to recapture those long-lost days of innocence grows too great). His younger brother will stay for longer,

A postcard showing AL6 E3122 arriving at Euston with the 'Manchester Pullman' c. 1969. Note the livery of the coaches, essentially a reverse of BR's corporate main-line passenger scheme.

thrilling still to the sight of a 'Deltic' powering along the East Coast Main Line or a 'Brush 4' taking a Freightliner to Southampton at speed. All the same, even he can't help feeling that the restless diesel on empty stock duties is more exciting than the AL6 at the head of the train.

Keith shows his ticket and heads down the long slope to the platform. He wonders why the Pullman has grey coaches with a blue stripe – the opposite of the usual BR livery. Marketing, he supposes. Everything seems to be about marketing these days. Stepping into air-conditioned comfort, he finds a window seat and drops the blind before settling down to his newspaper crossword. Confounded by Four Down, he gazes idly at the sports page until a steward politely invites him to take breakfast. *This is the life,* he thinks as the orange juice arrives. *This is what it's all about.*

Ten to eight comes: a route is set and a green light shines; a guard's whistle blows and a green flag waves; John 'notches up' and the loco wails into life. Passengers feel a jolt as the journey begins; on the platform a boy notes a number again. He watches as the train slips quietly away, while his brother grins at a girl in the last carriage.

* * * * *

The railway in 1969 was, in many ways, very different from the railway of 1950. Public ownership had been followed by modernisation and rationalisation as British Railways became British Rail and steam engines were replaced by diesel and electric locomotives. Yet the future came more slowly to some parts of the system, older practices limping on, and relics of former glories remaining in signs that sported regional colours, crockery that carried logos long since defunct, and hearts that stayed true to their old masters. This book records a twenty-year period which was challenging, exciting and surprising, and which ended with BR poised to bring high-speed travel to Britain for the first time.

NATIONALISATION: CATALYST FOR CHANGE

THE SECOND WORLD WAR moved many deceptively ordinary people to find the strength for bravery and selflessness. Norman Tunna, a shunter at the Great Western's Morpeth Docks, found both. During a massive air raid on Birkenhead on the night of 26 September 1940, he saw a flaming incendiary wedged in a wagon carrying high explosives. Leaping aboard, he freed it with his pole. The smouldering device fell to the ground, but as the woodwork burned on he sprayed it with a stirrup pump, before joining his colleagues at the water column to quell the remaining flames.

Tunna was awarded the George Cross, but there are countless other examples of railwaymen and women keeping calm and carrying on as they fought to run as regular a service as the conditions would allow. Such resolve earned rightful praise for the railways, but their efforts to get troops, military

BR experimented with various colour schemes before settling on Brunswick green for passenger engines, and black for mixed traffic and freight motive power. Sporting LNER-style apple green, Thompson L1 no. 67713 is seen at Liverpool Street in June 1948.

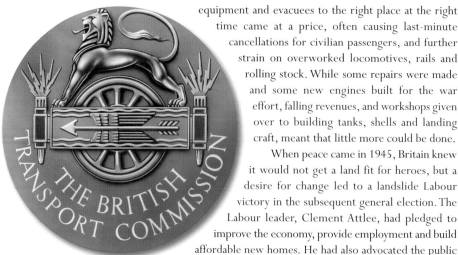

The official company seal of the British Transport Commission.

A map produced by BR in 1948, showing its original six regions. These would become five from 1 January 1967, when the North Eastern was absorbed into the Eastern.

equipment and evacuees to the right place at the right time came at a price, often causing last-minute cancellations for civilian passengers, and further strain on overworked locomotives, rails and rolling stock. While some repairs were made and some new engines built for the war effort, falling revenues, and workshops given over to building tanks, shells and landing craft, meant that little more could be done.

When peace came in 1945, Britain knew it would not get a land fit for heroes, but a desire for change led to a landslide Labour victory in the subsequent general election. The Labour leader, Clement Attlee, had pledged to improve the economy, provide employment and build affordable new homes. He had also advocated the public ownership of public services. As a result, the 1947 Transport Act heralded the nationalisation of the Great Western, London Midland & Scottish, London & North Eastern and Southern railways (along with fifty smaller companies) from 1 January 1948. To mark the event, locomotive whistles up and down the land cut through the darkness at midnight on 31 December. Some front-line staff feared for the future; others felt more optimistic; many 'old school' managers vowed to do as they had always done while the 'top brass' reorganised itself.

The system was divided into six regions (the Eastern, London Midland, North Eastern, Scottish, Southern, and Western), above which sat the Railway Executive, one of five that answered to the British Transport Commission (BTC). The BTC had been established to provide 'an efficient, adequate, economical and properly integrated system of public inland transport and port facilities within Great Britain for passengers and goods'. This meant that its first chairman, professional civil servant Sir Cyril Hurcomb, oversaw executives that controlled not only the railway, but also bus companies, road hauliers, docks, hotels, canals, tramways, shipping lines, and London Transport. The Commission even had its own film unit – British Transport Films – which produced some of the most innovative documentaries ever made.

The Railway Executive, trading as 'British Railways' (BR), inherited over twenty thousand locomotives, 56,000 coaches, a million wagons, 43,000 road vehicles, and almost nine thousand horses. The Labour Chancellor of the Exchequer, Hugh Dalton, described it as 'a very poor bag of physical assets', a remark that had a plangent ring of truth. Some of the tank engines in use on former Southern and LNER branches, for example, were in such bad shape that new LMS-designed locomotives had to be drafted in to cover the timetable, while overused, under-maintained points and plain line led to many speed restrictions, and even accidents – as at Wath Road Junction on 18 May 1948, when gangers failed to regulate expansion joints, allowing heat to distort the track and derail a passenger train; eight people died and many more were injured.

Whatever their state, the beleaguered railways remained as vital to the country as they were during the war. Sitting at your breakfast table in Bristol, Birmingham, Swansea or Stranraer, the newspaper in front of you, the coal in the grate and the marmalade on your toast would still have been brought by train – at least part of the way. As a 'common carrier', BR could refuse no consignment, so even that grandfather clock from Aunt Dolly in Harrogate would have come by rail to your town and by road to your door. And when the letters rattled through the letterbox, you knew the morning post was possible because the 'Night Mail' still crossed the border, its cargo still sorted *en route* by dedicated Royal Mail men.

Visits to aunts, uncles or the seaside would also be by rail. Air travel was only for the very rich; so was car ownership, but even if you did have a

The sun shines on no. 30203, as it shows off its pristine BR livery at Wadebridge. The engine was a member of the O2 class, introduced by the London & South Western Railway between 1889 and 1895.

The goods would get there, but progress could be slow, as 'pick-up' services fed into marshalling yards, where wagons were shunted into longer trains for long-distance transit. More marshalling and unloading would ensue before final delivery. At Glenfield, the shunter considers the next move while ex-Midland 3F no. 58247 simmers in the platform.

car, you probably wouldn't have enough coupons to fill the tank for a long journey; and with the British countryside still unscarred by motorways and dual carriageways, the whole thing would be such a mess of maps, minor roads and frayed nerves that you might as well get the train anyway.

The big stations could be sooty, the pre-war carriages tatty, the trains overcrowded, slow and bumpy, but there was little litter, and staff were attentive. Not all wayside stations were as well kept as the one at Titfield in the famous Ealing comedy (see page 55), but arriving for a branch-line train in Devon or Lincolnshire, you would doubtless have time to retire to a cosy waiting room after buying a ticket. Here, an idle moment or two could be enjoyed by the fire as the train wound its way across moors or fens, valleys or glens. With the signal clear, the guard would open a door to let you take a seat in an empty compartment. As you settled back into the comfortable upholstery, he would sound his whistle and the stationmaster would glance at his fob watch as a plume of smoke engulfed the platform.

Stationmasters were respected members of the community, but the driver was much more than that: he was a hero. His was the hand on the regulator, his iron will one-third of the alchemic mix of man, mineral and machine. Yet he relied on his fireman to create a good head of steam, and both relied on the signalman to keep the traffic moving safely, on the platelayer to keep the track in order, and on the train planner to create a smooth-running timetable in the first place. There was deference for one's superiors (nothing unusual about that back then), but also respect for one's elders, who would willingly pass on their knowledge, helping apprentices to grow in wisdom and understanding. Though rivalries between regions, depots and unions could be bitter, the kinship that had long been evident on the railway continued to bond those who served.

At the centre of this 'family' was the steam engine, loved by all – from driver to schoolboy, poet to R. A. Riddles, the dapper, charming Railway Executive member responsible for locomotive design and construction. Riddles, who had started his career with the London & North Western Railway in 1909, was no stranger to the footplate. He had volunteered as a driver during the General Strike of 1926, and had accompanied LMS Pacific no. 6229 *Coronation* on its 1939 tour of the United States, taking the controls himself for much of the trip (see page 52). At the Ministry of Supply during the Second World War, he had been responsible for the acquisition of motive power. This led to the introduction of two heavy freight classes, both of which saw service well into the 1960s.

New 'totems' started to appear on signs and stationery soon after nationalisation. Each region was allotted a distinctive colour: the Eastern had dark blue, London Midland maroon, Scottish Region light blue, the Southern green, and the Western brown. The North Eastern, however, received this rather startling shade of tangerine.

A local 'push-pull' service prepares to leave the bay platform at Midhurst, West Sussex. The station was built to the London Brighton & South Coast Railway's 'country house' design. Opened in 1866, closure was just under five years away when this photograph was taken in May 1950.

An ex-LNER Thompson B1 leaves King's Cross with a pristine rake of 'carmine and cream' coaches – a classic 1950s scene.

Riddles knew that many depots relied on relics of a bygone era. He knew too that the production lines of some of the major railway workshops were in full swing on a range of pre-nationalisation designs. By letting this continue, he could withdraw some of the oldest types that BR had inherited. Where motive power was concerned, Riddles had no faith in main-line diesels, believing the future to lie with electric traction. But electrification was clearly a long-term project, and practical solutions were needed quickly; his answer was to develop a suite of uncomplicated steam classes, which would feature shared components, and be easy to maintain, easy to operate and cheap to build.

Although no single Big Four locomotive stood head and shoulders above the rest, the resulting twelve types tended to favour LMS practice. Given the background of Riddles and his team, this was unsurprising, although LMS engines did enjoy a high availability rate and a certain degree of standardisation. The decision to take the Midland path was also shaped (to some extent) by the exchange trials that Riddles had initiated in BR's first year, and which involved the transfer of engines from each of the Big Four to other regions for assessment. While more useful results would doubtless have been reached in the new testing plant at Rugby (which opened in October

1948), the exchanges were good publicity and may have helped show locomotive superintendents that 'foreign' classes could perform as well as those they were used to – an important point to make when working on a range of engines for nationwide deployment.

The first 'Standard' to be completed was no. 70000 *Britannia*, which emerged from Crewe Works in January 1951. It was soon followed by fifty-four more – one of which (no. 70004 *William Shakespeare*) was proudly displayed as part of that year's Festival of Britain celebrations. The 'Britannias' were particularly welcomed by Eastern Region crews, who appreciated the improved timings they could achieve between Liverpool Street and Norwich, thanks to the locomotives' marriage of high power and low weight. London Midland drivers also returned favourable reports, while the Western's general dislike was contradicted by Cardiff Canton depot, which put them to good use on South Wales expresses. Very impressive they looked too at the head of a gleaming rake of brand-new BR 'Mark I' carriages, surging over the metals in this world of austerity and rationing. And yet their days were numbered almost as soon as they began.

In this optimistic Terence Cuneo painting, a brand-new 'Britannia' leaves Paddington with an express as an ex-GWR 'King' looks on. Though clearly of LMS parentage, the 'Britannias' incorporated best practice from a variety of sources.

FORGING AHEAD

BRITISH RAILWAYS   BRITISH RAILWAYS

THE FIRST BRITISH RAILWAYS STANDARD EXPRESS LOCOMOTIVE

MODERNISATION: PLANS AND DREAMS

I T's STILL DARK as Bill Fleming arrives at Bath Road shed in the city of Bristol. He's in good time for his six o'clock start, and makes his way to the small cabin where some of his fellow cleaners are waiting. A few are trying to doze; others are looking at yesterday's paper; most are chatting about this and that. As Bill takes a swig of tea from his can, the door opens and the chargehand comes in to take his teenage workforce off to the stores for cotton waste, cleaning oil, rakes and shovels.

Today, Bill's first job is to clear out the boiler tubes of an old Great Western 4-6-0. It's dusty, dirty work, and not as much fun as rubbing down a smooth boiler casing, or polishing the brass beading round a nameplate. But Bill knows that if he does a good job the engine will steam more efficiently and be a credit to the railway he loves. The shed foreman thinks he has the ability to become a fireman, and has said so. Bill is delighted and hopes one day to 'pass out' from fireman to driver, just like his father had done for the old company.

A job on the railway was a job for life. Yet with Britain enjoying full employment (or something very like it) by 1953, BR soon found it hard to attract new recruits, as fewer and fewer men wanted to get covered in soot and grime cleaning, firing and maintaining locomotives – despite what some of them might have thought as boys. Steam locomotives demanded a great deal of looking after and could take up to two hours to prepare for traffic, even after the boiler had been filled and the fire lit. True, they were built from indigenous materials and powered by indigenous fuel, but recent coal shortages, price rises and concerns about quality had weakened this benefit somewhat, and had even led to a brief flirtation with oil firing. Add in growing concerns about pollution and the parlous state of BR's (and Britain's) finances, and it was clear that the BTC had been right to suggest a study be undertaken to assess the relative advantages of steam, diesel, electric and gas turbine traction.

Electrification combines low running costs with high acceleration, allowing intensive services to be operated. This makes it especially attractive

Opposite: Of the twelve 'Standard' classes, arguably the most successful was the 9F 2-10-0, introduced in January 1954 for fast and heavy freights. Here, no. 92045 passes Hendon with a coal train in March 1955. Some 9Fs also worked passenger services, notably on the Somerset & Dorset line.

'Big Four' experience had shown diesel shunters to be more economical than their steam counterparts. Despite uncertainties about main-line diesel traction, the Railway Executive largely agreed. More than one hundred locomotives had been delivered by 1953; many more would follow.

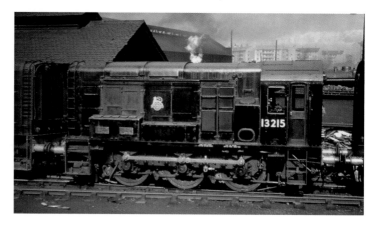

Bill Fleming's domain – Bristol Bath Road shed – was still home to many ex-GWR steam locomotives when this photograph was taken in May 1952.

for concentrated commuter lines, as the Southern Railway had found when it completed its conversion of the London suburban network in 1929. The LMS and LNER also inherited and developed various schemes, although the latter's Liverpool Street–Shenfield route was 'switched on' under BR in 1949. Its scheme to raise the wires between Manchester, Sheffield and Wath – stymied first by economic crisis, and then by the outbreak of war – finally came to fruition in 1955, but hopes for a fleet of fast diesels to serve the East Coast Main Line had been dashed by the Executive with some speed after nationalisation.

In fact, diesels were no strangers to Britain, shunters and railcars having been used by various companies since the 1920s. Even so, steam remained dominant, and it was not until the end of the Big Four era that engineers started to think about putting internal combustion engines to main-line use. A few orders were placed before nationalisation, but only no. 10000 – a joint venture between the LMS and English Electric – emerged before 1 January 1948. By the mid-1950s, BR had taken possession of six further locomotives. Together, this small pool was eyed with suspicion by some railwaymen and many enthusiasts, who believed that anything diesels could do steam could do better. The BTC disagreed, but trials continued rather half-heartedly, Riddles and the Executive preferring to press on with their 'Standards' for use where electrification could not be afforded.

The public at large was oblivious to these rivalries, happy instead that the travelling experience was beginning to improve as new coaches replaced some of the old, and track repairs started to let expresses be run at higher speeds. Now City businessmen could reach Bristol in 105 minutes, just like they had before the war, and grandparents, sisters, brothers, lovers and others could catch 'The Elizabethan' from King's Cross and arrive at Edinburgh Waverley a mere 6½ hours later. This 'non-stopper' featured in a cinema short made by British Transport Films (1954), where a 'long journey gilded by the sun' is stretched to celebrate the whole rail system – from the wheelwrights and maintenance gangs responsible for the smooth ride to 'the Howards, the Berts, the Cynthias, the Mabels' enjoying it. But behind the smoke and compartment mirrors, the narration is elegiac, and when the train slows for a red signal the spell breaks and the dream disperses. It was a prophetic moment, for the fact was that – as standards of living improved – more people were choosing their Morris Minors and Austin A30s (and the apparent freedom they brought) over the

'The Elizabethan' was a non-stop King's Cross to Edinburgh Waverley express that ran from 1953 to 1962. Power was usually provided by an ex-LNER A4. In this 1953 scene, no. 60032 *Gannet* heads through York with the up service, watched by the photographer's young family.

By 1955, there were over three million cars on British roads. BR's fears about road competition would be well founded, but passenger receipts still rose by £2 million in 1959. In this contemporary view, a group of holidaymakers arrives at Weston-super-Mare in Somerset

A leaflet produced by the British Transport Commission to outline its Modernisation Plan programme for 1956–7.

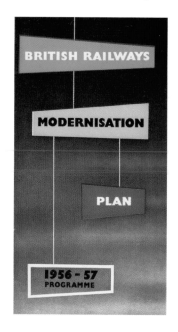

train. This, coupled with rising operating costs, began to turn BR's surplus into a deficit.

Unhappy with how the figures were falling – and the BTC's over-bureaucratic structure – Winston Churchill's new government produced a Transport Act in 1953 that abolished the Railway Executive and allowed the Commission direct contact with the regions, which suddenly found themselves with new powers. This led to an unnecessary proliferation of diesel multiple unit designs, as orders were placed to local specifications – although onlookers often marvelled at the surface veneer, some named trains seeing a restoration of liveries that recalled the Big Four days of yore. However, the Act also denationalised the road-haulage industry, launching a sell-off of over twenty thousand lorries to private firms, which could offer prices that undercut the railway – something that increasing numbers of freight customers exploited. (Many who did so during the two-week rail strike of 1955 would never return.) Nevertheless, BR continued to compete by replacing old-fashioned yards with a smaller number of mechanised ones, where palletised goods were shifted by fork-lift trucks, cranes and conveyor belts, instead of armies of muscle-bound men.

Some of these measures were brought about by the drive for modernisation led by General Sir Brian Robertson, who had taken over from Cyril Hurcomb in September 1953. A distinguished army veteran of two world wars, Robertson saw the railway as a public service that he was duty-bound to deliver to a high standard. He soon established a modernisation committee, which published its findings at the end of 1954. The so-called 'Modernisation Plan' was supported by the government, which set aside £1,200 million of public money to be spent on it over fifteen years. The aim was to 'exploit the great natural advantages of railways as bulk transporters of passengers and goods and to revolutionise the character of the services provided for both'. With Riddles having retired, and technology having moved on, this 'revolution' would not only involve mechanisation, more colour-light signalling, and permanent way improvements, but also the substitution of steam by diesel and electric traction. The Plan recognised that much 'useful experience' had been gained with the designs BR had inherited, and asserted that 'in view of the high degree of reliability attained in other countries where diesel traction has been widely adopted, there is no reason to doubt that equally satisfactory results will be realised here'. A 'Pilot Scheme' was developed to test various power levels, wheel arrangements and transmission systems, orders for around 170 locomotives being placed in November 1955.

Diesels were cleaner than steam, required less maintenance and were ready for action at the touch of a button – or they were when they worked. Fires, flashovers and failures were not uncommon, while some simply seemed to lack the requisite horsepower. The sudden influx of new traction types could also be hard on drivers, some of whom now had four, five or six different diesel classes with which to familiarise themselves. Depots, too, felt the strain as the training programme cut the number of crews available to work their normal services and the number of artisans on shed to keep things running. On top of this, many men hated being confined to the cab after the freedom of the footplate, and loathed the loss of dignity they felt in the new 'open-plan' multiple units. Passengers, on the other hand, loved the panoramic forward-facing views they afforded – encouraged no doubt by the many films and posters that advertised the fact.

Although later years would see a growing band of diesel enthusiasts take pleasure in the variety that the Pilot Scheme created, the truth was that far too many different locomotive types were purchased. Indeed, government pressure on BR to clear its deficit more quickly than envisaged led to further orders being placed before any of the original batch had

In 1951, the Railway Executive appointed a committee to assess the use of lightweight diesel multiple units on branches and cross-country routes. The first trains began to appear in 1954. This publicity shot shows a Park Royal example arriving at Buckingham in 1957. Note the LMS signage still *in situ* some nine years after nationalisation.

This 1957 view of Sheffield Victoria shows ex-Great Central D11 'Director' no. 62663 alongside EM1 electric no. 26052. The EM1s were based on an LNER prototype and worked passenger and freight services over the Woodhead route until 1981.

Pilot Scheme success. English Electric Type 1 D8000 stands on display at Battersea Wharf on 30 June 1957, twelve days after delivery to BR. In all, 228 locomotives of this design would be built, production resuming after its superiority over the proposed 'standard' for the 800–1,000hp power range (the Clayton Type 1 – see page 39) had become apparent.

even been delivered. Some would only just outlive the steam classes they were meant to usurp. BR's electrification plans, on the other hand, would be rather more successful – particularly after the optimum power supply method had been ascertained.

The Southern Railway had favoured a 750-volt direct current (DC) passed through a third rail to the train's traction motors via 'shoes' attached to the bogies. The Woodhead line between Manchester and Wath was also powered by DC, but at twice the voltage and via overhead line equipment (OLE). Riddles, however, had been impressed by French railway experience with alternating current (AC) at 20kV; one of his final acts as a railwayman was to initiate trials of fifty-cycle AC traction on the Lancaster–Morecambe–Heysham line. While the SR would continue with third-rail DC, this experiment – and a survey of the Euston–Manchester–Liverpool route – confirmed that AC at 25kV (to which the French had converted in 1953) offered significant economies in the size of the contact wire and OLE, the number of substations required, the power distribution arrangements, and the clearances that would have to be provided for bridges and tunnels.

An experimental prototype was followed by five 'test' classes, which – like their diesel counterparts – were produced by a number of builders, including BR itself. Lessons had been learned from the wasteful

Pilot Scheme failure. Twenty Metropolitan-Vickers Type 2s were built between 1958 and 1959. They proved so unreliable on the 'Condor' – BR's Anglo-Scottish express freight service – that customer demand dropped until alternative traction was provided. D5711 is seen at Disley with a Derby service c. 1960. Withdrawal for the entire class would come within just eight years.

Pilot Scheme, however, and this time BR imposed certain requirements, such as the basic body shape, axle load, weight restriction, and wheel arrangement. The first of the new breed entered traffic in November 1959; electric services began between Crewe and Manchester in 1960.

The Liverpool Street–Southend line and the Glasgow suburban network were other beneficiaries of electrification at this time, while Glasgow was also to enjoy the advantages of the signalling upgrade programme, a new signal box opening at Central station in January 1961. Mechanically operated signals and points require local control, as the force needed to shift the signal levers outweighs the signalman's strength the further the equipment lies from the box. Conversion to electric operation allowed a wide area to be worked from one place, while the regularly spaced colour-light signals that went hand in hand with the scheme allowed more trains to be run at higher speeds. This was good for business, but modernisation is not always driven by economics or politics: sometimes, safety concerns step in. BR's Automatic Warning System (AWS), for example, had been designed to help prevent stop signals from being inadvertently passed at danger. In October 1952, soon after trials had begun, its need was demonstrated when an express passed a red signal in fog at Harrow & Wealdstone. It struck the rear of a commuter service, before a third train ploughed into the wreckage. In all, 112 people were killed. AWS was introduced between King's Cross and Grantham in 1956. By the turn of the decade, it had reached York and was spreading to other routes, as it joined the modernisation of maintenance, marshalling, locomotives and rolling stock in building a safer and more efficient railway. The future seemed bright, and would continue to do so. For a while.

THE BEECHING YEARS

A SOLEMN CROWD gathers at Swindon Works. Ahead of them lies a shining green locomotive; behind them, over a hundred years of history. Today, something is ending. Is it a tradition? Job security? Or just a way of life? *Still, as someone says none-too-quietly, it's not as bad as when the last Great Western engine left the shops – this one's an untidy looking thing...*

No other product of man's mind has ever exercised such a compelling hold upon the public's imagination as the steam locomotive. No other machine in its day has been a more faithful friend to mankind nor has contributed more to the growth of industry ... Ladies and gentlemen, I now unveil this locomotive and christen it the *Evening Star*.

The Chairman's speech was as stirring as the name was fitting: after *Evening Star*, no more steam engines would be built for British Railways; soon, their

Opposite:
Chalford station, on the Gloucester to Swindon line, was on Beeching's 'hit list'. Having lost its freight traffic in August 1963, passenger services followed in November 1964. Here, an ex-GWR 'Pannier' prepares to depart for Gloucester a couple of months before the end.

Left: *The last of the line.* After a rousing speech by R. F. Hanks (chairman of the BTC's Western Area Board), 9F no. 92220 is named *Evening Star* at its birthplace, Swindon Works, on 18 March 1960.

Delivered to BR in 1959 and put into service on the Western and London Midland regions over the next two years, the luxury 'Blue Pullmans' featured air conditioning, sound insulation and at-seat attendance. In this view, a Midland unit makes a test run past Chapel-en-le-Frith in 1960.

numbers would start to fall; soon, smart electrics would serve the suburbs, diesel-powered 'Pullmans' would whisk passengers to Manchester or Bristol, and the route of the 'Flying Scotsman' would resound to the gunboat drawl of the 'Deltics'.

In 1953, the BTC decided to test a pool of locomotives with hydraulic transmissions, in order to measure performance against diesel-electric machines. The Western, which had little experience of electrics, readily agreed to host the trials. Having arrived at Paddington, a 'Warship' class diesel-hydraulic rests as passengers alight, taxis wait and – rather disconcertingly – an ambulance stands by, sometime in 1961.

Yet the transition was not a smooth one: the beautiful Glasgow 'Blue Trains' had a tendency to catch fire, forcing steam to be substituted on some services, while the folly of ordering so many untested diesels was growing ever more apparent, as an embarrassing number found themselves waiting in sidings for engine replacement later in the decade. Elsewhere, work was only just starting on a new marshalling yard at Carlisle; that it would take 2½ years to complete – at a time when freight traffic was dwindling – summed up for many the Modernisation Plan's distance from reality. Alarm bells were starting to ring, not least in Whitehall.

The 1959 general election had returned the Conservative Party to power. The following year, Prime Minister Harold Macmillan told the House of Commons that 'the railway system must be remodelled to meet current needs, and the Modernisation Plan must be adapted to this new shape'. In an odd marriage, Macmillan, a former director of the Great Western Railway, put his faith in Ernest Marples, a road-engineering contractor involved in motorway construction. To avoid any conflict of interest, the new minister divested himself of his shares in the Marples, Ridgeway company – to his wife, as it turned out. In the years ahead, he would be accused of impropriety and much more. Either way, he might justly be described as a 'pro-road' transport minister.

The production version of English Electric's 'Deltic' prototype began to appear in 1961. In all, twenty-two were built to replace steam on East Coast Main Line expresses. Their 100mph top speed allowed services to be accelerated considerably. Here, D9005 attracts admirers at York in September 1962.

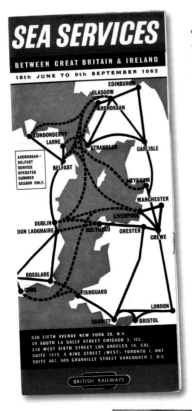

Although passenger receipts rose by £2 million and operating costs fell in 1959, a recession in the steel industry two years later hit BR's freight business hard. The Commission had no means of offsetting the £90 million deficit that had accrued by this time, but it had been trying to save money by expanding its fleet of multiple units and railbuses, and by closing loss-making lines (like most of the old Midland & Great Northern route between Peterborough and Great Yarmouth). Robertson still believed in the Modernisation Plan and wanted to forge ahead with it; Marples disagreed and appointed a special committee – headed by the chairman of Tube Investments, Sir Ivan Stedeford – to find ways of reducing its expense (*inter alia*). The committee felt that BTC thinking had focused on engineering matters too much. Its proposals, therefore, led to the cancellation of some electrification schemes (including the Coventry avoiding line), the reversal of the decision to fit all wagons with continuous brakes, and the scrapping of centralised signalling on the

Below: A publicity booklet for the newly electrified Glasgow suburban network, featuring a painting by Terence Cuneo. Despite early teething problems, the 'Blue Trains' soon settled to give sterling service. Featuring pneumatically operated doors, and large windows, they proved popular with passengers until final withdrawal in 2002.

Above: BR inherited a number of ships from the Big Four and continued to operate ferries to the Channel Islands, the Isle of Wight, France and many other destinations. This timetable for 1962 provides details of the 'sea services' available between Great Britain and Northern Ireland.

Nuneaton–Crewe route (which meant the retention of around twenty smaller signal boxes – although the signals they controlled were upgraded to electric colour lights). Robertson criticised the cuts, commenting on the 'chasm of difference' between his view of the railway as a public service and the government's idea of it as a mere transport competitor. But Robertson was due to retire at the end of May 1961, and the appointment of a Stedeford Committee member as his successor was a clear sign that Whitehall meant to follow the commercial path.

The cigar-smoking Dr Richard Beeching was more relaxed than Robertson, and courteous almost to the point of being friendly – not exactly usual for the time. As a director of ICI, he also had the sort of sharp business brain that Marples sought, although such virtues came at a price: part of the deal was that Beeching's ICI salary would be matched; this brought him £24,000 a year – £14,000 more than Robertson, and £10,000 more than the Prime Minister. However, for this he was expected to deliver a solution to a problem that had persisted since the nineteenth century: making the railways pay.

Beeching knew this issue could only be addressed after deep analysis of the figures. By the end of 1961, he had mandated a thorough study to assess

In 1962, BR had twenty-eight workshops in operation. All were well-versed in steam technology, but experience of modern traction was limited. BR's Workshop Plan, published that same year, outlined a programme of rationalisation and modernisation. Swindon Works, seen here in the mid-1960s, was one of those deemed suitable for retention.

British Railways

Passenger travel
and map folder

This travel leaflet and map from *c.* 1962 lists some of the services available to passengers, who were able to arrange (*inter alia*) sleeping-car berths, 'camping coach' holidays and transport for large parties.

which traffic ran at a profit, which ran at a loss, which lines made money, and which existed only through subsidy. He also set about simplifying Robertson's complex management structure of 'generals', committees and sub-committees, opting to recruit private-sector experts in a move to bring financial – as opposed to military – discipline to the Commission. Further simplification came with the 1962 Transport Act, which abolished the BTC and established a British Railways Board (BRB), with powers to set passenger fares, and more freedom with freight rates than hitherto. Beeching became its first chairman on 1 January 1963. Two months and countless cigars later, Her Majesty's Stationery Office published *The Reshaping of British Railways*, which set out his plan to put the railway 'in the black' by 1970.

Beeching understood that the industry had emerged from the war in 'a poor physical state' and that its economic situation had steadily worsened since. He understood too that the Modernisation Plan failed because it did not predict 'any basic changes in the scope of railway services or in the general mode of operation of the railway system': the BTC had simply expected the abolition of steam, concentration of marshalling yards, mechanisation of goods depots, centralisation of signalling, and so on, to cut costs and attract more traffic. And though BR had lost its 'common carrier' status, Beeching felt the company was still 'heavily influenced' by it, focusing on wagonloads (which involve much transhipment and shunting) instead of trainloads (which involve little or none). Road hauliers were much cannier about selecting the most lucrative work; BR, on the other hand, took *anything*, even if – like Aunt Dolly's grandfather clock – it yielded no profit.

Beeching told cinema audiences that, while he knew profitability was not the only measure of value for a public service, 'the real question' was 'whether you, as owners of the railways, want us to go on running these services at very high cost, when the demand for them has very largely disappeared'. He thought not, and advocated 'radical changes', suggesting that the replacement of steam be accelerated, stopping passenger services be cut, and loss-making stations be shut.

Between 1949 and 1962 the BTC had closed some 3,000 miles of 'unremunerative' lines, but it was Beeching's plan to close 6,000 miles more that drew most attention from the press. Many television and newspaper reports of the period featured protest marches, 'last rites' ceremonies held as trains departed little-used stations for the last time, and villagers telling of the hardship that would come with the withdrawal of services. Some of the most vociferous objectors who arrived to tie wreaths on smokebox doors came by car, but others were loyal passengers who risked losing their jobs when the allegedly dense bus network failed to serve their (and their employers') needs.

Dr Richard Beeching in affable mood, c. 1963.

The trouble was that Beeching's income figures were based on receipts issued at a particular place. This painted a blacker picture for stations more likely to be journey's end than journey's source – such as a seaside resort. He also failed to see that branch lines contributed traffic to the core network, overestimated the ability of rail to win general merchandise consignments from roads, and assumed that passengers who had lost their local station would simply drive to the nearest main-line one, when in reality many would make their entire journey by car. Yet the report included many constructive plans, such as the 'liner train' concept, which involved the movement of containerised goods in dedicated 'express' services, and the block movement of coal in wagons that could be loaded and unloaded in motion. Both ideas would come to beneficial fruition, but Beeching's bad press overshadowed both the positive side of his first report and virtually all of his second, *The Development of the Major Railway Trunk Routes*, which appeared in February 1965. Here, he set out to show how rail traffic could be concentrated and further investment justified in a bid to develop 'a new railway out of the old'. This was not original either, but management problems had prevented the BTC from making any progress. Beeching's calculations of what BR's passenger and freight requirements were likely to be in 1984 led him to conclude that, of the

In the late 1950s BR began experimenting with four-wheeled diesel railbuses in an attempt to cut operating costs and encourage patronage on its minor branches. In this view, W79976 stands at Tetbury, which – unlike some – continued to lose money. The station was earmarked for closure by Beeching and finally succumbed on 6 April 1964.

7,500 miles of main-line railway, only 3,000 'should be selected for future development'.

The Doctor's forecasts are easily discredited with hindsight (as forecasts often are), but it could equally be argued that he was trying to build the business in the shape of increasing competition from road and air. The latter had become a particular worry, domestic airlines having begun to entice significant numbers of passengers away from Anglo-Scottish services. Beeching believed that, by concentrating traffic on single routes, the 'route cost per unit carried' could be reduced, and the railway could be made more viable. Unfortunately, his language could be ambiguous, which made his reassurances that the 'unselected', duplicate trunk routes would not be closed seem dubious, especially when one of them – the Great Central line through Leicester, Nottingham and Sheffield – had already been 'condemned' in his first report.

The part played by politics is a recurrent theme in railway history, and soon Beeching would find himself condemned: by the time *The Development of the Major Railway Trunk Routes* appeared in print, Labour had been returned to government. Victory for Harold Wilson brought defeat for Beeching, disagreement with the new regime leading to his return to ICI the following June.

Although the swingeing cuts managed only to contain BR's deficit, history still remembers Beeching as the 'axeman'. In fact, his legacy was much wider, and included new staff appraisal schemes, improved training programmes and up-to-date management methods. It also included a new image.

British Railways – with its dark greens, maroons and browns – had started to look a bit 'old hat' by 1964. As a result, Beeching gave the company's design team a clear brief to create a sleek, businesslike identity, which would help bring confidence and cohesion to the network. That May, its initial efforts were revealed when the experimental 'XP64' train was released from Derby Works. Featuring new carriages with smarter interiors, better soundproofing, pressure ventilation, and improved suspension, its most eye-catching element was perhaps its livery: a shade of turquoise blue matched with light grey, quite unlike anything that had gone before. The train was hauled by a new Brush Type 4, finished in the same blue, but with one important addition – there beneath each cab, on a temporary red background, was a symbol that remains with the railway to this day. The final version of the new scheme was revealed at an exhibition in London during January 1965, along with new uniforms, new signage, a new alphabet, and a new name: *British Railways* was part of the past – the future belonged to *British Rail*.

The shape of things to come. A publicity shot of the XP64 train, featuring D1733 and the 'arrows of indecision' (as many detractors dubbed the new logo). Introduced in 1962, over five hundred of these 2,500 hp locomotives would be built by 1968. They could be found on passenger and freight duties across Britain. Many survived into the twenty-first century.

A LAST BREATH
OF STEAM

A couple enjoying the splendour of their first-class compartment, c. 1966. By now, BR had adopted the continental twenty-four-hour clock, meaning that passengers no longer caught the 'Night Ferry' to Dover at nine, but at the seemingly incomprehensible 21.00.

BEECHING'S REPLACEMENT was Stanley Raymond, a long-term public servant whose impatience and ruthlessness were well known to colleagues, not least on the Western Region, which he had managed before his rise to the Board. A proud man, he was in some ways a product of the new emphasis on business brought in by his predecessor – an emphasis that forced many older managers to curb their enthusiasm, especially if – *heaven forfend!* – it included the ownership of a large model railway. The time for 'playing trains' was past, for there were new traditions to be built in 1965.

Raymond had a clear vision of how the railway should be developed, and did not accept road and air competition as a *fait accompli*. He was keen to

hone BR's marketing strategy, and strove to create a nationwide 'brand' with a clear identity. Thus in 1966, 'Motorail' became the new name of BR's car-carrying passenger service and 'Inter-City' became synonymous with comfortable, crack expresses. That June, the BRB tried to speed the homogeny by decreeing that all motive power be painted in its new livery. Yet beneath the blue surface most would still admit to being LNER men, LMS men, or even Great Central or Cambrian men at heart. These old retainers were more 'white heat of the firebox' than 'white heat of technology', but the withdrawal of steam had accelerated to such an extent that some depots found it hard to muster enough engines to haul all their allotted services. Thankfully, diesel reliability was improving as BR built more bespoke depots, with their comparatively clean conditions, and artisans became ever more adept at dealing with their new charges.

The peak year for steam locomotive withdrawals had been 1962, when almost three thousand were taken out of service. Among them were the ex-GWR 'Kings', which dated from 1927, but now some of the BR 'Standards' were going too. The average lifespan of a well-maintained steam locomotive

Below: Rebuilt Bulleid 'Battle of Britain' no. 34071 (formerly named *601 Squadron*) stands at Waterloo after arrival from Weymouth in 1966. Though the nameplate is missing, the fire burns on – but will only do so for one more year on the Southern.

Above: Electrification of the Crewe–Liverpool Lime Street section of the West Coast Main Line was completed in January 1962, after which the wires went up towards London. This leaflet was published in 1966 to mark the start of BR's full public timetable of electric-hauled Inter-City services from Euston.

was around thirty years, so scrapping anything under ten years old (as plenty would be) seemed like a terrible waste, despite the apparent economic and operational reasons for doing so.

The first region to rid itself of steam was the Western, but the last to use it on express passenger trains was the Southern, which had come closest to Riddles's ideal scenario, withdrawing engines as it electrified area by area. While the third rail was being laid alongside the Waterloo–Bournemouth route, most trains thus remained in the charge of Oliver Bulleid's mighty Pacifics.

Like the Chief Mechanical Engineers of the other Big Four companies, Bulleid had remained in office after nationalisation; before retiring in 1949, he experimented with double-decker electric trains, 'mock-Elizabethan' tavern cars, and the 'Leader', an ambitious steam engine with cabs at each end like a diesel. All these developments were controversial and, ultimately, unsuccessful. Not so the Pacifics, which – while expensive to work and maintain – were highly impressive; those rebuilt in the 1950s enjoyed increased efficiency, leaving Southern Region managers sure they would be able to handle most traffic needs until electrification was complete.

Modernisation was gaining pace by 1967, with new liveries appearing on trains, new uniforms on staff and new posters on billboards and bridges. Many stations nevertheless retained their traditional benches, barrows and

Passengers await their trains at Waterloo in 1966. The clock in the background was – and is – a popular meeting place.

signs. At Waterloo, this meant kaftans and miniskirts mingling with kiosks and flower stalls, while the old departures board cackled at faces focused on *Vogue* or the latest Len Deighton.

Ignore the shopping precinct of the twenty-first century, and imagine waiting beneath the clock at *this* Waterloo for a train to Bournemouth or Southampton, a pink carnation in your buttonhole, a copy of *The Times* under your arm...

A diesel hums at the head of an Exeter express, an electric glides in from Portsmouth, but haunting whistles and barking exhausts reign supreme. Steam pervades the air as a 'Standard' tank brings in a long rake of coaches. The shunter, who's been hanging about by the ticket gates, disappears between the buffers to uncouple, before a huge Pacific glides past her platform-end admirers to 'hook on'. Like many engines of this period, her green paint is caked in soot and grime, bar a small patch on each cabside, which the driver has rubbed with cotton waste to reveal the number: 35007, a 'Merchant Navy' once named *Aberdeen Commonwealth*, but whose nameplates – like many others – have been removed for safe keeping by staff, enthusiasts or persons unknown. With the signal clear and the 'right away' given, the locomotive struggles hard to move the train up the grade, its driving wheels slipping, its connecting rods flailing as the sun reflects off the white discs on its bufferbeam.

For many Southern drivers, the summer was tinged with the chill of autumn: they knew the end was coming, and the final fling they enjoyed – with

The Clayton Type 1 was supposed to be the standard design for its power range. Unfortunately, the locomotives were demonstrably inferior to their English Electric counterparts (see page 24); withdrawals began in 1968, just six years after introduction. Here, D8586 arrives at Stirling in August 1965.

A final fling. Rebuilt Bulleid 'Merchant Navy' no. 35007 *Aberdeen Commonwealth* powers through Deepcut Cutting on 1 April 1967. The white headcode discs (as opposed to oil lamps) denote the type of train being worked – classic Southern practice. Towards the rear, BR's new carriage livery is starting to usurp the traditional green.

bearings worn, regulators opened wide, and coal shovelled on by the hundredweight – resulted in logbooks full of astonishing performances. Many steam buffs, photographers and home-movie enthusiasts relished the sight of the old engines as they thundered past, their green retinue broken only by the odd flash of blue and grey. The magic 'ton' was reached on several occasions, but when no. 35003 *Royal Mail* touched 105.88 mph between Winchfield and Fleet as it worked a train from Weymouth on 26 June, it was the last time a steam locomotive performed such a feat in Britain.

By now the 'Bournemouth Belle' had switched to diesel traction, but there were hopes that a 'Merchant Navy' might be reinstated for the last-ever service, which was to be worked on Sunday 9 July. Sadly, management thought otherwise, and a Brush Type 4 took charge, leaving steam to bow out on a nondescript parcels train. The new order took over on Monday morning, but while electrification brought sleeker services and higher passenger numbers, it also condemned Southern spotters to a diet of bland multiple units. These slab-sided rakes did little to stir the blood. They weren't even especially new: the SR had chosen to base its front-line trains on the 1950s 'Mark I' carriage at a time when the other regions were taking delivery of new 'Mark IIs' (although the units were more up-to-date than the forty-year-old Tube stock that had replaced steam on the Isle of Wight, it had to be said).

The distance between past and present was opening out into a battleground: preservation societies were on the increase, and the whole

After the withdrawal of steam, Waterloo–Bournemouth services were taken over by electric multiple units like this one, seen at the Dorset resort on 8 July 1967.

movement was starting to grow teeth. BR's intention to 'develop' King's Cross and St Pancras (which would result in the destruction of at least one architectural gem) was a case in point: having failed in his bid to save Euston's Doric Arch earlier in the decade, John Betjeman was quick to join the anti-demolition campaign; after a year of negotiation, St Pancras attained a Grade I listing in November 1967. Yet BR had to look ahead, and somewhere in an office in Derby, a team of designers was working on a passenger train that promised to be a total revolution.

The Southern was not devoid of diesels. Among its fleet were ninety-eight Type 3s, which were delivered from BRCW between 1960 and 1962. Nineteen were later fitted with equipment that allowed them to push and pull carriages on the non-electrified Bournemouth–Weymouth route (among others). Here, D6517 passes St Denys in June 1967.

THE NEXT TRAIN

'We're going to stop Beeching in his tracks!'

S O SAID LABOUR CANDIDATES on doorsteps and at meetings in the run-up to the 1964 General Election. When the Party took office later in the year, however, it seemed that this promise would be broken – there was no reprieve, after all, for the Somerset & Dorset, whose end would come in March 1966, and whose signalmen would polish their brass instruments on the very last day in a display of defiance...or pride...or both.

The S&D's was a story repeated at many other signal boxes, stations, sheds and goods yards. But as the demolition trains were making their way inexorably across Britain, Barbara Castle – who took over as Transport Minister in December 1965 – was sparing a small number of lines where roads were inadequate or inappropriate for development. The logic behind her decisions was shaped in the coming months and galvanised in the seminal 1968 Transport Act, which set down principles that would safeguard loss-making – but socially valuable – lines and place the railway on a real public service footing. To further this aim, the Act also wiped out BR's accumulated debt of £153 million, and established Passenger Transport Executives (PTEs) in and around Greater Manchester, Glasgow, Merseyside, Tyneside and the West Midlands. The PTEs would co-operate with BR to provide local bus and rail services, and would be encouraged by government to integrate the two (much as the BTC had tried to do until Marples came along).

Stanley Raymond had helped form many of these ground-breaking strategies, but he was not destined to see them published during his tenure. Unofficially, he did not get on with Mrs Castle; officially, she felt the new policies would give BR 'fresh terms of reference involving a different outlook in matters of finance and long-range planning'. Such changes, she said, required a corresponding change of leadership. Raymond was left with little choice: his resignation was immediately accepted, and he was gone by the end of 1967.

The Times speculated that Peter Parker, then director of food wholesaler Booker McConnell, would take over; his time would come – but not yet.

Opposite:
Stanier 8F no. 48652 stands by at Bolton on 20 April 1968. The engine is showing off a hand-painted number plate on its smokebox door.

Overleaf, top:
A Gloucester Railway Carriage & Wagon diesel multiple unit arrives at Hooton with a train for Helsby in March 1967. As a result of the 1968 Transport Act, this station would come under the aegis of the Merseyside Passenger Transport Executive from 1 January 1969.

Below: Derby was not only home to the technical research department: railway workshops had existed here since 1840, and continued to build steam and (later) diesel locomotives like this one well into the 1960s. Sulzer Type 2 D7672 was just two months old when photographed sporting the new BR livery in April 1967.

The new man at the top was Henry Johnson, a career railwayman who had started his working life with the LNER, and who went on to become General Manager of the Eastern and London Midland Regions. Popular with staff, he was a true motivator and enjoyed a good working

relationship with the Ministry. He also had a greater grasp of engineering matters than all who had gone before him, although he could be cautious about new ideas.

Oblivious to this, BR's Research Department at Derby had developed the concept of an Advanced Passenger Train (APT), which promised speeds of up to 155 mph, and the ability to minimise passenger discomfort by tilting into curves – an enormously exciting prospect that matched the space-age optimism of the era. The project secured partial government funding in 1968, and clearance to construct a four-car experimental train the following year.

Many APT staff had come from the aerospace and aircraft industries. The advantage of this was a certain freedom from traditional railway engineering precepts; the disadvantage was a lack of useful experience, which led to many mistakes, meaning that tests often had to be rerun and purchase orders re-raised.

The 'old guard', less impressed with the 'youngsters' and their new-fangled ideas than the 'youngsters' perhaps were with themselves, saw that an alternative was possible. In early 1969, they made a strong case to the BRB for a 'High Speed Diesel Train', which could reach 125 mph and would feature a new design of luxury carriage, boasting greater capacity, a corresponding reduction in the number of vehicles required and (therefore) in maintenance costs. Johnson saw their point and gave the 'HSDT' his public

Old freight at Kingmoor. Rakes of goods wagons roll into this Carlisle marshalling yard. After a nudge over the 'hump' by a locomotive, their speed and route will be centrally controlled until they come to rest in a pre-ordained siding.

A poster from 1968, showing a young couple reunited by Inter-City.

support, adding that if the APT did not prove itself within the next four to six years, BR would need something reliable to fall back on.

For the railway and its future customers, this was the tipping point of change. In the twenty years since nationalisation, BR's route mileage had shrunk from 20,000 to less than 11,000, staff numbers had dropped from nearly 650,000 to 296,000, and wagon numbers had fallen from over a million to 430,000. Indeed, freight had perhaps come the furthest. The Modernisation Plan had foreseen the growth of container traffic, BR testing the water at the end of the 1950s with its 'Condor' and (later) 'Speedfreight' services. Beeching took the idea forward with the liner concept, which – while successful – made many new marshalling yards redundant. Around eight hundred yards were closed, but while Freightliner established itself as a national network (and had even extended its reach to France and Belgium), BR felt there was still much business in the sundries market. In 1969

New freight at Kingmoor. By 1967, block trains were starting to replace many traditional goods services. 'Brush 4' D1858 is seen passing the yard with a southbound 'Freightliner'.

its unremunerative small-consignment collection and delivery service was transferred to a new National Freight Corporation – a helpful move, but if BR were to compete on a serious level, it would have to reorganise the way its rolling stock was managed. The computer system that could deliver this was on the way, but in the meantime sales activity was damped down until service quality could match the quality of the new air-braked wagons that were coming on stream.

Elsewhere, plans were being made to compensate for Pilot Scheme over-ordering by reducing the diesel fleet from twenty-eight classes to fifteen, while the Automatic Warning System, continuous welded rail and colour-light signalling were spreading further across the network. In passenger terms, this brave new world found a focal point in the 100mph West Coast Main Line, which was enjoying increasing passenger numbers, and which had – as the publicity material proudly proclaimed – brought London, Manchester and Liverpool closer to the heart of England. And yet, as state-of-the-art diesels took plush expresses on from the electrification limit at Crewe, they passed through the last enclave of steam …

At the start of 1968 there were over 350 engines still at work in north-west England. Enthusiasts flocked to the area to be beguiled by 'Black Fives' on local services and 8Fs on freights, while soulless 'blue boxes' whizzed by on the main-line. And they *were* just blue boxes to some: steam had

The other face of the Inter-City era. Work-weary 'Black Five' no. 44828 leaves Skipton with a Morecambe–Bradford (Forster Square) service, corporate-liveried coaches in tow.

Train of the past. Although there is no official headboard, this is the famous 'Farewell to Steam' tour of 11 August 1968, better known as the 'Fifteen Guinea Special'. 'Britannia' no. 70013 Oliver Cromwell is just backing on to the train at Manchester Victoria, having taken over from 'Black Five' no. 45110.

personality – steam engines *breathed*, and attracted as many admirers on the job as off it. Now old drivers reminisced about that battle over the moors with a mineral train, while firemen told how smoke seemed to linger about engines that had been 'dead' for a month, as they waited in weed-strewn sidings for their final trip to the breaker's yard.

Timetabled steam haulage ended on 4 August, after which the last sheds – Lostock Hall (Preston), Rose Grove (Burnley) and Carnforth – closed their doors for good. Many locomotives were in a terrible state by this time. Some enthusiasts had done the best they could with cleaning oil and rags; some had even spruced up red bufferbeams and reinstated missing nameplates with a paint brush. Others found that the layers of grime responded well to chalk, and chose instead to adorn grey tenders and boilers with unofficial slogans like 'Steam lives' or 'Steam forever'. But nothing lasts forever, and it was left to BR's expensive 'Farewell to Steam' special to close the chapter in style.

At 09.10 on 11 August, 'Black Five' no. 45110 eased a train of railway lovers and steam buffs out of Liverpool Lime Street and headed for Manchester Victoria. Here, the 'Five' was replaced by a resplendent no. 70013 *Oliver Cromwell*, which took over until Carlisle. When the train returned to Liverpool later that day, children cheered, women waved and men wept (or perhaps they'd just got something in their eye?). For BR management, steam was old-fashioned and inefficient; from January 1969, even preserved engines would be banned from its metals.

Train of the present. A brand-new state-of-the-art diesel-electric at the head of a rake of blue-and-grey coaches. The locomotive was one of a fleet of fifty introduced in October 1967. With the end of steam, all traction types were reclassified in readiness for future computer operation. This English Electric Type 4 thus became a Class 50.

As trainspotters and enthusiasts mourned, travellers knew the modern railway was ideal for going Inter-City to Glasgow, Manchester, Bristol or Cardiff. Not so ideal, maybe, if you were heading to Midsomer Norton, Hawick or Sidmouth – though not everything had changed. Sitting at the breakfast table with Radio 1 blaring from the wireless, the newspaper in front of you would still have been brought by rail. The coal in the grate may have come by other means, but the kettle and the toaster worked because more trains were making their way day after day from colliery to power station, unloading their carboniferous cargo automatically from high-capacity

BR began operating light hovercraft services to the Isle of Wight in 1966. Two years later it took delivery of the first SRN4, which could handle 250 passengers and thirty cars. Named *The Princess Margaret*, the craft worked between Dover and Boulogne under BR's new 'Seaspeed' brand.

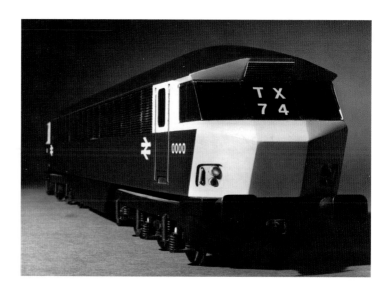

Below: The winter sun streams onto a steamless scene as Class 47 D1863 and Class 55 D9003 *Meld* wait at King's Cross in December 1968.

Above: Around 1969, BR was testing ideas for the next generation of heavy freight locomotives, which would be capable of exerting 6,000 horsepower at speeds of up to 125 mph. This model shows how the finished machines might have looked had the project continued.

hopper wagons. By this time, Aunt Dolly's grandfather clock would have been collected by a yellow National Carriers Ltd van, which would have taken it to a depot for dispatch by train or — more likely — lorry via Britain's growing motorway network. But when the letters rattled through the letterbox, you knew the morning post still relied to some extent on 'Travelling Post Office' trains and the skill of their staff.

Technology was attracting more business, the 1968 Act had provided financial stability, yet many people were now opting to drive all the way, take a road coach or catch a plane. BR had fought back with Inter-City, Motorail, and even an agreement with Godfrey Davis to provide car-hire facilities at major stations. But it knew the war was far from won. In July 1969, the next salvo came in the form of a design exhibition at the Haymarket. Amid the displays of innovation and invention in its hotels, stations and sleeper services was a full-size mock-up of a new carriage interior and an extraordinary model of the APT. BR claimed it would help make the 1970s 'a decade of progress such as railways have never seen'. Everyone, it seemed, was waiting for the Next Train.

BR's 'Next Train' exhibition of July 1969 featured this futuristic model of the APT; a stylised version also appeared on the cover of the accompanying brochure.

51

PLACES TO VISIT

MUSEUMS

Barrow Hill Roundhouse Railway Centre, Campbell Drive, Barrow Hill, Chesterfield, Derbyshire S43 2PR. Telephone: 01246 472450. Website: www.barrowhill.org Britain's only surviving, operational roundhouse engine shed.

National Railway Museum, Leeman Road, York YO26 6XJ. Telephone: 01926 621261. Website: www.nrm.org.uk Home to many preserved locomotives, including Stanier Pacific no. 6229 *Duchess of Hamilton*, which swapped identity with no. 6220 *Coronation* for a 1939 tour of the United States (see page 15).

STEAM: Museum of the Great Western Railway, Kemble Drive, Swindon, Wiltshire SN2 2TA. Telephone: 01793 466646. Website: www.steam-museum.org.uk

Thinktank, Millennium Point, Curzon Street, Birmingham B4 7XG. Telephone: 0121 202 2222. Website: www.thinktank.ac Home to no. 46235 *City of Birmingham*

HERITAGE RAILWAYS

A number of Britain's heritage railways use locomotives, rolling stock and infrastructure that were built, manufactured or used throughout the 1950s and 1960s. Some even host events themed around the era. Details may be found in various books and magazines, as well as on the Heritage Railway Association website: www.heritagerailways.com

Of particular interest are:

Great Central Railway, Loughborough, Leicestershire LE11 1RW. Telephone: 01509 230726. Website: www.gcrailway.co.uk The only double-track heritage line in Britain.

Isle of Wight Steam Railway, The Railway Station, Havenstreet, Isle of Wight PO33 4DS. Telephone: 01983 882204. Website: www.iwsteamrailway.co.uk Experience island rail travel as it was before many lines were closed and former Tube trains took over the Ryde–Shanklin route.

Llangollen Railway, The Station, Abbey Road, Llangollen, Denbighshire LL20 8SN. Telephone: 01978 860979. Website: www.llangollen-railway.co.uk Operates a variety of steam and diesel locomotives, along with several first-generation diesel multiple units.

The Midland Railway, Butterley Station, Ripley, Derbyshire DE5 3QZ. Telephone: 01773 747674. Website: www.midlandrailwaycentre.co.uk

The Midland Railway Trust's large collection includes many diesel locomotives and multiple units from the BR era.

North Yorkshire Moors Railway, 12 Park Street, Pickering, North Yorkshire YO18 7AJ. Telephone: 01751 472508. Website: www.nymr.co.uk This line runs through *Heartbeat* country and offers occasional 'Sixties' events, which include period locomotives, road vehicles and live music.

Strathspey Railway, Aviemore Station, Dalfaber Road, Aviemore PH22 1PY. Telephone: 01479 810725. Website: www.strathspeyrailway.co.uk Steam and vintage diesels through the Highlands from Aviemore to Boat of Garten.

Swanage Railway, Station House, Railway Station Approach, Swanage, Dorset BH19 1HB. Telephone: 01929 425800. Website: www.swanagerailway.co.uk Home to many Bulleid Pacifics such as saw the end of Southern steam in 1967.

West Somerset Railway, The Railway Station, Minehead, Somerset TA24 5BG. Telephone: 01643 704996. Website: www.west-somerset-railway.co.uk 26-mile heritage line through the Quantocks.

A couple waiting for the next train at Reading, c. 1967. The map shows the 'Road-Rail Link' coach services which began that March between the station and Heathrow Airport. This connection between flights and fast Inter-City trains became increasingly useful as cheap package holidays grew in popularity.

FURTHER READING AND VIEWING

This book is intended to be a sketch of British railway history in the first two full decades after nationalisation and is not, therefore, an exhaustive survey. More detailed information may be found in the following volumes:

Bonavia, Michael R. *British Rail: The First 25 Years.* David & Charles, 1981.

Boocock, Colin. *Spotlight on BR: British Railways 1949–1998 – Success or Disaster?* Atlantic, 1998.

Bryan, Tim. *Railways in Wartime.* Shire, 2011. The 'prequel' to this book.

Fiennes, G. F. *I Tried to Run a Railway.* Ian Allan, 1967. Includes insights into the introduction of the 'Deltics', the genesis of BR's 'merry-go-round' coal trains, Beeching's failure to consider rationalisation as a way of increasing the viability of loss-making lines and the problems of constant reorganisation. Fiennes' criticism of BR management policy led to his dismissal by Beeching's successor, Stanley Raymond.

Gourvish, T. R. *British Railways 1948–73: A Business History.* Cambridge University Press, 1986.

Gwynne, Bob. *Railway Preservation in Britain.* Shire, 2011. The concurrent story to the main-line saga.

Hardy, R. H. N. *Steam in the Blood.* Ian Allan, 1971. Growing up with steam, working with steam, and keeping steam going during the era of modernisation.

Hardy, R. H. N. *Beeching: Champion of the Railway?* Ian Allan, 1989. A more sympathetic view of the Doctor.

Haresnape, Brian. *British Rail 1948–1978: A Journey by Design.* Ian Allan, 1979. Covers the design development of locomotives, rolling stock, coach interiors, uniforms, ferries, stations, typefaces, and so on.

Henshaw, David. *The Great Railway Conspiracy: The Rise and Fall of Britain's Railways Since the 1950s.* Leading Edge, 1991. An in-depth study of railway closures and political meddling.

Johnson, John, and Long, Robert A. *British Railway Engineering 1948–80.* Mechanical Engineering Publications Ltd, 1981. The engineering story, told by engineers, and edited by former BR Chief Mechanical Engineer R. C. Bond.

Wojtczak, Helena. *Railwaywomen: Exploitation, Betrayal and Triumph in the Workplace.* Hastings Press, 2003.

Wolmar, Christian. *Fire and Steam: A New History of the Railways in Britain.* Atlantic Books, 2007.

Plenty of photographic albums featuring BR in the 1950s and 60s are also available, while most of the source documents referred to in this book – including the Modernisation Plan and the Beeching Report – may be downloaded free of charge from the Railways Archive website: www.railwaysarchive.co.uk

The British Film Institute has released a number of British Transport Films' finest documentaries on DVD. They are available from a variety of online and high street stores. Other films available on DVD include:

The Titfield Thunderbolt (1953) – the fictional story of a successful attempt to save a rural branch line.

The Ladykillers (1955) – includes several railway scenes shot in and around King's Cross.

A Hard Days' Night (1964) – the first Beatles film, which features many on-board scenes.

Black Five (1968) – this film commemorates the end of steam in the north-west of England; the DVD includes *The Painter and the Engines* (1967), which details artist David Shepherd's work at Nine Elms during the final months of steam on the Southern.

INDEX

Numbers in italics refer to illutsrations